What We Have in Common

A Brim Coloring Book
Written by Jane Landey
Edited by David Austin

Drawings by David Austin and Jane Austin

Copyright©2017

Published by CreateSpace: An Amazon Company.

Printed in U.S.A.

Introduction

What We Have in Common. Brim Coloring Books enable children color the drawings as they read along! The series display the similarities of related animals.

In this series Weka and Kiwi are compared. The facts enable children to appreciate common values.

Thus, imbibing in them interest towards animals which could help them appreciate what they have in common with one another.

The Weka

And

The Kiwi

Weka and Kiwi are two small birds without wings. They have no tails and cannot fly.

A weka and a kiwi meet by the way side.

I am a kiwi.

I am a weka.

I cannot fly.

I cannot fly either!

I lay eggs.

I lay eggs too.

I like to eat fruits.

I like to eat fruits too!

I keep my young ones around me.

Me too!

I walk about searching for water.

So do I. Water is important!

I can run fast!

I can run fast too!

And I live in the forest.

I live in the forest too.

Well, I have two legs and a long beak.

I have two legs and a beak too!

I can peck wood to search for ants to eat.

I can peck wood and look
for ants to eat too!

My long beak gurgles water quickly.

My sharp beak gurgles water quickly too! Water is important for both of us.

I look like a chick!

Me too!

I have a way of swallowing food
quickly.

I swallow food hurriedly too!

I can hide under a leaf and no one can see me!

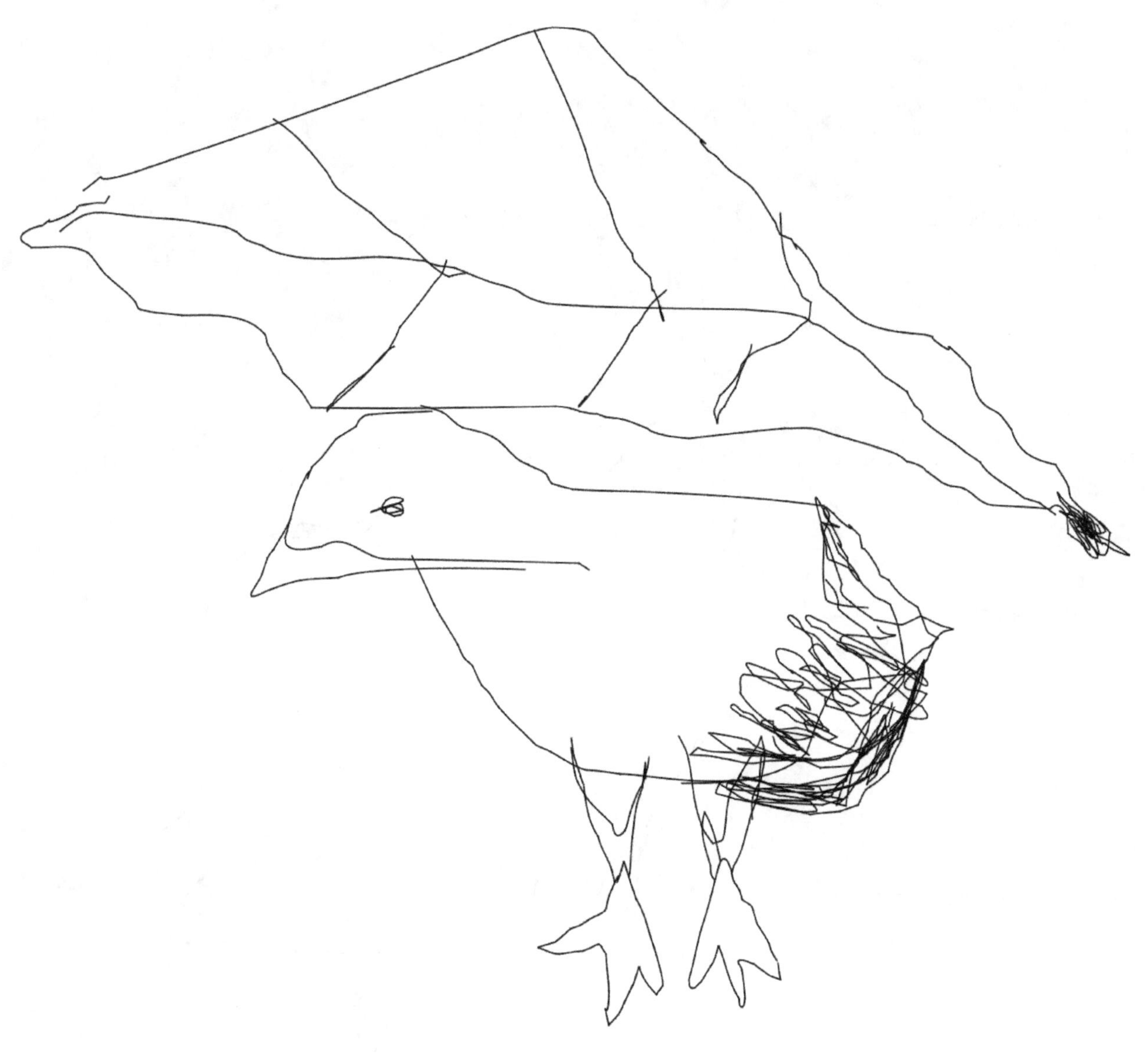

I can hide under a leaf too!

Do I look bigger than you?

Not really, but maybe.

So stand by my side.

I am bigger than you! Bye.

What We Have in Common Brim Coloring Books

Crocodile and Alligator
Turtle and Tortoise
Starfish and Octopus
Worm and Snake
Turkey and Vulture
Ostrich and Emu
Weka and Kiwi
Bat and Rat
Camel and Llama
Duck and Pelican
Kangaroo and Wallaby
Pig and Tapir
Skunk and Squirrel
Hedge and Anteater
Cat and Owl
Elephant and Rhinoceros
Dog and Fox
Buffalo and Bull
Leopard and Cheetah
Horse and Zebra